Descent

poems by

Jennifer LeBlanc

Finishing Line Press
Georgetown, Kentucky

Descent

ACKNOWLEDGMENTS

These poems, sometimes in different versions, first appeared in the following
journals.

The Adirondack Review: "Noon," "Pulse," "To the Man I Left"
CAIRN: The St. Andrews Review: "Divine," "First Night," "The Laugh," "A
Love Poem," "Poem for My Young Cousins," "The Wanting"
Cannoli Pie: "Answers"
The Main Street Rag: "Ghazal of the Virgin Mary," "Girl Reading a Letter"
Melusine: "Elizabeth"
The Penwood Review: "Place du Vieux-Marché"
Subliminal Interiors: "Irish Window," "Matryoshka Dolls"

I am deeply grateful to my family and friends, especially Mom, Dad, Kristina,
and Ashley, whose patience and unwavering support allowed me to see this
book to completion. To Julia Lisella, my teacher and mentor, thank you for your
invaluable guidance. And to Dave, for always being there, *je t'aime*.

Publisher: Leah Maines
Editor: Christen Kincaid
Cover Art: Cover painting: *The Abduction of Europa* by Rembrandt Harmensz.
          van Rijn. Digital image courtesy of the Getty's Open Content Program.
Author Photo: Edward Hayes Photography
Cover Design: Elizabeth Maines McCleavy

Printed in the USA on acid-free paper.
Order online: www.finishinglinepress.com
          also available on amazon.com

Author inquiries and mail orders:
Finishing Line Press
P. O. Box 1626
Georgetown, Kentucky 40324
U. S. A.

Table of Contents

A woman like that is misunderstood.
I have been her kind.

—Anne Sexton, "Her Kind"

Without

Her lips stitch, a taut thread.
Did you used to play with dolls?
As though posing plastic limbs would have
made me maternal, as though combing
false hair could have turned some key in me,
a secured lock, could have opened a purse.
Nana smooths the wide afghan that blankets
her mind, folds back this new corner
and tries to understand the woman she finds
sleeping on the bed like a young nun
released of her habit, a woman alone.

Wave

Before I could tell
that desire is purpose, I used
to wade out off the coast

from the rented house, pull
my arms and legs slow through
the water-tug and hoist

myself up, onto a rock.
Summer again, ten years later.
I sit on the porch with

my cousin and her child.
There is no *she*, one self facing
the other. *She* is the same *she*

feeding the other, eating
what the other mashes into lunch.
The ultrasound pulses

in its picture frame shell—
even there it moves—another
coming for her soon.

I bounce my foot, cross
my legs, tilt a glass of soda
until the liquid drains away.

I lean on my elbow.
When the baby cries,
I pretend that I could help.

Ballot

Night uncurls like a cat and bats
a dream, a mouse, from the sky.

In the house, she tests her odds
at tossing loaded dice on a black cloth.

The wrong sides always come up
just when she thought she found luck—

a groove of cool wind on the hottest
day when spiders shrivel in their webs.

Another woman cuts her hand on glass,
a shallow splash of milk in the sink.

The cat sighs as temperatures rise.
She flushes the wound of its blood.

Mother and Daughter

But what happens when the mother is taken
away, brought under, masked with anesthesia?

The daughter sits in the waiting room
in a chair that seems too large, wide.

She passes the operation hours
reading and writing her worries—

what ifs and *remember tos.*
What happens when the parent

does not fall in love, but is consumed
by depression? Hades is clever,

knows how to separate daughter
from mother, mother from daughter.

It makes no difference to him—
he just needs someone to share hell with.

Operation

When Mother goes to the underworld
through the needle of anesthesia, seeds hold

her for some time and then release her
back up. Underworld slaves row her

stretched on crisp sheets,
bed wheels churning the floor.

When she comes up for the first time,
it is in dream. *How does one dream*

when these seeds are caught in the veins?
Eight seeds rise and crack open

releasing saccharine blood.
When she comes up, returned

to Daughter, she mumbles what the dead
understand, what Daughter must.

Seasons

Daughter turns the seasons
of *daughter* and *woman*. Which she prefers
depends on the moon, what Mother plants
in the garden, who comes to visit.
Daughter is familiar—a dress comfortable
to wear, pearls circling her neck, fair skin,
powder to prevent sweat that summer morning when
her cousin married and the whole family danced.

Woman is where she is headed—cotton sheet
draped over her shoulder at night, window open
to insects and rain, wind through the birch tree,
mist rising from the street she can see
·by lamplight. She imagines a man at her side,
her hand on his rising chest.

Pleasure

More and more Daughter sleeps
and when she dreams it is of Hades.
She remembers little in a summer's space,
Mother overwhelming her with bright flowers
and trees green with health of nature,
distractions to remind her that earth is *home,
birthplace, where she belongs.* When autumn
comes, under the comforter on her bed,

she covers her shoulders and summons
the underworld, damp cling of spider webs,
Hades' hand clamped around her
shoulder and how he says, *This way,*
and she follows, settles into her skin.
No need to be rational.

Divine

Sing the early morning.
September coming, the window lifted.
Ask for the divine and I will
hold up my palm, nothing
to offer, waiting for a coin.
Every autumn the ache returns,
sweet cider snapping in my mouth
            like a kiss
and I want to be taken
            back into his love.
Am I wrong for it?

In the sharp apples,
in the still-green fields—
            he, he—
in the mist-wet porch swing,
in the early moon,
in the out-from-storage wool—
            he, he—
in the hair I give to the wind.

First Night

We wake to the gray morning,
to the dim November light.

I am still in your arms.
Somehow, you have kept

hold of me. What comes after
our first night, after I hear myself sigh

when you move your hand
down my arm. Even in sleep,

you know how to love me.
Tom Waits sang us to sleep.

Song after song, you whispered,
This is a pretty one, this one, too,

and I believed you.

A Love Poem

Because the couple at the bar held hands,
the blond and the man with the Irish tattoo,
because the doorway was narrow
and reminded me of a needle's eye,
because we stepped over the threshold
and the train took us into the night
of the tunnels and the bell sounds,
because of the white numerical statue
and the granite mermaid,
because of Nikola Tesla
and his gentle pigeon love,
I broke my promise to you,
I said it again.
        I want to share
        this bright, messy life.

Discovering

Though no one can ever know,
I don't think he has a face.
                    —Anne Sexton, "For Eleanor Boylan Talking with God"

You pace the halls of heaven
waiting to find out, waiting to see,
fur coat wrapped around your shoulders,
you hold a poem in your hand.
Under the watch of curious angels,
you walk from stand to stand
(I imagine heaven has podiums)
and mark your lines with revisions
until it is time to meet him. Or her.

I like to think that God is a small,
young woman—the girl in Burton's
Dreams who rests on a green pillow,
her chemise draped from her arm,
and purple flowers, not poems,
in her hand. Let her be our god.
Let this girl cup Anne's chin
in her palm, let her send the world
spinning with firm delicateness.

Inside a Waterborne Canoe

This is how I want to die—
as clean as soap. I want to see
animal clouds, sun meeting

the pond-sheen. Let my hand rest
on Sexton's *Collected*—stand-in
for the Host—my tongue

curled around truth,
thumb pressed to tough,
sweet fruit. The sun is warm

in its night-room.
Let the fish un-mute
their trumpet mouths.

This is how I want to die—
one hand stretched
up to find the moon.

Trespasses

*In ancient Rome, if a Vestal Virgin abandoned her chastity, she was
buried alive.*

He entered me
and I felt the low notes
of a morning choir slide like fire
through my bones. I closed
my eyes against the ladder
I knew I would climb down,
down into this underground room.
The priest turns and sunlight shuffles
and shuts as attendants shovel earth
over this death-hut. Then it is cold.
There is bread and water,
oil next to my bed. No. I will not eat.
I lie down against the pillow and arrange
my hands, torso, legs, feet. In the dark
above me, I see his face. I trace
his silhouette with the tip of my tongue.

Descent

I.

The man who once, years ago,
was almost my lover, lives alone in the city
three blocks down from the train.
I would like to drive my car out from here,
find his door. *See, I saved myself for you.*
I saved myself for you. What is it to save?
Doomsday is coming and by the end of the year,
some think we'll be dead, all of us burned
or blasted into fine particles like grains of sand
unless we prepare. They stock guns and save
cans of food on ceiling-high shelves.
I would like to ask what he has saved.
I would like the room to be dark. I would like
to lie down at his side and not move.

II.

To lie down at his side and not move.
This morning on my way to the mailbox,
a great blue-black bird with a wingspan
wider than I thought could be true
snapped its talons from brittle grass
and flew across the marsh.
To be like that, rising,
intermittently falling, gliding
and then settling down,
pulling close the feathers. I imagine
each thread, each bristle on the wing.
To offer that sort of flight,
to kiss the forehead like
a blessing.

III.

A blessing,

my first blood came
when I was not too young,
not too old, had not been waiting
long, testing to see if it started.
Best, it came at home.
Russet on white cloth. I remember
a cold draft from the bathroom
window and snow on the screen
like flour—fine, granular matter.
I thought about Vestal Virgins,
how they could hold water in sieves.
Not so much the impossibility, I think,
but the balancing with no reprieve.

IV.

Balancing with no reprieve
their chastity against desire.
A Vestal's punishment for sex—
live burial. Imagine being pressed
into the underground room with a bed
for a tomb, water and food so she would
not starve. Who would eat the bread
set out on a board? Who would tip a glass
of water to her lips? I would like to know
what most did before death, how a voice
sounds under earth packed as tight
as though its mouth never opened.
Who repented, and who blamed
the man who once was her lover?

Ghazal of the Buried Vestal

I line each bone of my spine against the bed,
press my hands, damp with anticipation, against the bed

and wonder how long it will take me to die. I am a great
sinner, a woman who brought a man to her bed

and thought, like a star, her innocence
could be snuffed out but still shine. In this bed,

no one repents. No one sends *sorry*
up through the mound of dirt hiding this bed

from a man who might pass, might shovel back
the earth. It is cold in this underground bed.

I wanted them to send my lover down with me.
They handed me fire instead, this lamp next to the bed.

Leave-taking

A manual on how to ruin something dear:
Drive down the dirt road. Let him shield
          your view from the deer—

dead, strung up like meat in a market,
hooves clasped. His hand will not let the deer

distract from your grasp on the wheel.
Listen when you hear shots. *Hunting deer.*

We should have worn orange. Forget talismans
when you bring someone to the mountains,
          someone dear.

Instead, concentrate on the sting, the ease
of leave-taking. Put your thumb on his pulse.
          Kiss me slow, dear.

To the Man I Left

December 31st

I need to become used to seeing you as my victim.
For so long, you were the man who trespassed against me.
The deer will be let down during the New Year celebration.
Men will drag the carcass to the woods. No one will see.

For so long, you were the man who trespassed against me
and I was the deer shot through with a biting bullet.
When they drag the carcass to the woods, no one will see
the changed face on the deer, the metamorphosis.

I have made you the deer shot through with a bullet,
the ammunition stamped with *She loves him, she loves him not.*
The changed face on the deer, the decadal metamorphosis
allowed the hunter to press his finger against the shot.

The ammunition was stamped with *She loves him, she loves him not.*
You held up your hand so that I could not see the deer.
The hunter pressed his finger against the shot.
I should have held down your hand, seen the creature.

You held up your hand so that I could not see the deer.
The deer will be let down during the New Year celebration.
I should have held down your hand, seen the creature.
I need to become used to seeing you as my victim.

Cardinal-Red

The summit was barren, one great stone and dead trees.
We hiked the mountain to see the foliage. The dormant trees

turned up brown leaves and bare, reaching branches,
arms held up to us, an offering from the trees

that could not offer much. *If you want children,*
but I do not.... You photographed the trees

while I stayed on the great stone, that cold
bed in the middle of the summit where the trees

turned around me, the center of a world.
You wanted autumn for your camera, cardinal-red trees.

Pulse

The mountain whose name means bright,
      round fire overhead,
rose on our right until we turned
      and found the deer—dead.
Does it matter that I have said
you shielded my view from the deer,
      animal with hooves raised
and head thrown back? Here:
      I take away my love.
What happens to my thumb against your pulse?
What happens to the presentation of my mouth
turned up as a weed would reach for heat?
      It matters that I have promised
to tell the truth. I have said this—
we climbed the mountain whose name means bright,
      we left our brilliance there.

Noon

Noon is the hill you climb with the man you used to know.
Noon is the summit of the hill where you know

you will leave him because of this: noon is different
from evening. One is the pond you never see but know

is around the corner. The other is the window
        that acts as mirror. You know

he can see himself if he turns his head to the left.
One is static. The other changes with what you know

is called perspective. A man leans over a woman
and asks if she is alright. She knows

that she will leave him. She says yes.
This is evening, kissing him instead of saying
        what you both, instinctively, know.

Metaphors

She was a cardinal
        that tapped the window
            for food,

scratched the glass with terri-
        ble persistence, then
            flew to

another pristine feed-
        er. The seeds were gold
            manna.

Can you blame a bird whose
        feathers are fawn? She
            is the

needle when thread is pulled
        through cloth. Red of de-
            sire,

red of hurt. Can you blame
        a woman whose hair
            is short,

wind permitted through the
        window at four. Gold
            manna

static on the counter,
        cheesecloth-covered jar.
            She was

a coat brought out from stor-
        age, the hanger—her
            shoulders.

New Leaf

The night he told me the names
he has chosen for his future children,
we went to a Saudi Arabian film
about a girl who wants a bicycle,
and her mother, first wife of a man
who is intent on having a son,
new leaf to pin on the tree.
Wadjda, the girl, does not count.
He told me the names in the car,
and I told him what I would call our children,
as bland in name as they are in my mind,
the children I do not want.
We held hands in the theater.
I traced my thumb across his palm at the dialogue,
He was the first man in my life,
and I hope he will be the last.
We held hands in the American theater,
and later, in his bed, I was amazed
by our luck at not being Saudi Arabian,
no need to fear the *mutawa*.
Our relationship was over
in four days when I told him no,
I would not have the children.

Exposed

For the foot the glass cut
sudden   what comes next
what comes after water-rush?
I loved that quickly once.
It was autumn and the hurt
was not bad   a thin
veil lifted from the chest
the soft saying of the word
fuck   the corner table.
A child heard and I was
embarrassed for the man
who said it   whom I loved.

Blue Thread

Waving to me across the years,
        your starched white formal shirts,
                our tongues touching. I watch

the birds scatter in an arc as sharp as
a curse. If I read the creases on your sleeves,

the lines become grenade pins.
        The streets become stoning sins,
                blue thread from a burqa.

Blue thread from a burqa,
        the streets become stoning sins.
                The lines become grenade pins,

a curse if I read the creases on your sleeves.
The birds scatter in an arc as sharp as

our tongues touching. I watch
        your starched white formal shirts
                waving to me across the years.

In the Waiting Room

After Elizabeth Bishop

The dentists found the cadavers and searched the mouths
for gold crowns, pressed gloved fingers between the lips

and cheek and tongue and tooth, loosened the gold.
The story can be heard in the waiting room

and it is bright and night does come early in New England
and this winter, the *Geographic* reports on art in the Congo.

There are still the horrible bodies, a woman wearing oil filters
over her breasts and with motor oil slicked onto her arms.

I am still not over my ex, and it is a blue, blue winter,
each night the sun going down fast and the mail carrier

at the metal box, open, shut, like a valve in the heart.

Matryoshka Dolls

The body of the ancestor is as ornate
as the largest matryoshka doll in the nest.
The imagination is prepared to picture her veil
worn to church, the rouged shape
of her mouth from which another language came,

certainly not the same tongue
found on the doll three steps down
which is the grandmother
whose plaid dress is almost as simple

as the mother's solid apron.
The mother is understood well
and is immediate to the empty shell

that is the daughter that does not open,
who I am and will continue to be.

Irish Window

In response to an aerial photograph of Inishmore from David Lyons' Ireland.

Green panes of stained glass—the pastures,
the fields separated by stone walls

that resemble raised lines of brown metal.
Limestone as purple as a saint's

removed heart and a patch of grass
with lavender patterned like petals.

A road cuts down the middle
as though fire divided the glass

and then someone set the halves together—
connected although cracked.

Elizabeth, Daughter of Immigrants

O land of opportunity, you are
not the suppers with meat, nor
the curtains with lace nor the unheard of
fire in the grate on summer afternoons
                    —Eavan Boland, "The Rooms of Exile"

I am sure the lace curtains
were still that day, that
winter afternoon in
Waltham, Massachusetts.

The fire in the grate
would have simmered down.
Small coughs of ashes.

The dinner meat browning
on the kitchen stove
in the next room

when my great-great-aunt
drowned her two daughters
and then ran outside
to unburden the news.

Oh, Mrs. Kelly,
what have I done?

Her mouth red
and throat burning
from the lye she drank.

Elizabeth

Born 1897, died 1926

I.

I shake the pill bottle like a rattle
and spill the beads, line them
along my collarbone, roll to the side
and watch them scatter on the sheet.
I am mesmerized by this pearl-heap—
treasure-hold of sleep-gold
that fails to bring me dreams.

My husband leads our girls to bed
and tucks them in with kisses,
sweet-dream wishes.
The blessing on their pillows is sleep.
My sleeping pill is white.
It is a splendid pearl.
I turn, toss although burned
by the white teardrop,
the water cup sloshing
and leaving a wet ring
on the nightstand.
Handkerchief swirl.

II.

Philip loves me
and wrestles my fears,
dares to smooth my hair
when I clench my fists.

When I clench my fists
and bare my teeth against the world,
he whispers—*Betty, listen*
to the wind outside the pane.
Hear the wind chime
dance, a metal bird.

Perhaps the metal bird
is my heart. I settle against
the pillow and sleep until
the sudden peacefulness scares me.

My heart pounds.
I slept through another dinner,
another bath for our children.
Philip sings them to bed
with sweetness on his tongue.
He does this for me

although I am ugly,
submerged in my own past
and my own madness.

III.

I see dead rats in the toilet.
I'm one of the lunatics.
Bibles flap open
like broken birds
until Mother tells me
birds are curses
and won't I hold still?

I would, but the rats in the toilet
call me *broken bride.*
This cannot be!
I stood at his side
in a white dress
that scratched like mice
raiding the sugar cabinet.

Mother locks the cupboards,
complains I grow fat on pastries
and jams. Enough of that.

She should know it's the mice
who nibble the sweets,
then swell into rats
with bird talons for feet.

The Laugh

In response to Pierre-Auguste Renoir's The Swing.

The tree, his straight spine, the blue
ribbons that climb my dress. One foot on the swing,
I balance on my heel. This is weighted.
Is that always how you laugh?
Heat goes off in my head like an alarm
and the child starts a nervous dance.

Charles tries to ignore the dance,
the child spinning in a circle, blue.
Blue pinafore, red mouth chirping alarm
as would a small bird. Does she want the swing?
She mocks me with a better laugh.
My laugh is weighted

like a stone in the throat, weighted
like a controlled impulse or dance.
I hold down the bad laugh,
straighten my white dress and its blue
ribbons. I focus on the swing
under my foot, concentrate against the alarm.

This is a persistent alarm.
It rises in a fine sweat. I am weighted
with too many questions, thoughts that swing
in and out of view like a dance
seen through a narrow lens, nervous blue
vision. This is how I laugh.

The child stops spinning. Her laugh
is gone and silent. She watches my alarm,
watches these looped blue
ribbons pull me down. Shoulders weighted,
I do not move in a smooth, calm dance,
but falter a little on the swing.

The ease of being this swing.
No one asks it for a better laugh.
I want to stretch. I want to dance,
move away from this hot-bellied alarm,
but I am a doll in this dress, weighted
like a glass vase and its blue

hue. I used to dance with the alarm
of a good laugh, none of this weighted
trembling on a swing, moving in the blue.

Ghazal of the Virgin Mary

When a messenger descends from the shelf of heaven to earth,
the woman who receives him feels sharp shock from the earth.

Each morning, I slice another curl from my head
until the bedroom floor looks as though spirits from the earth

sprouted thumbs with dark fur and curled up.
I leave them there. I watch men harvest from the earth

grains as golden as coins. I watch sheep
that live in small pens eat these riches from the earth.

I know something about nourishment, beginnings, birth,
new life drawn from an older body, not from the earth.

Before my son died, he called me *Woman.*
Mary means *bitter*, a dark root drawn from the earth.

The Annunciation

The shudder of air pulsing—
moths beating against light
on round-moon nights.
The ground convulsing

with fright—lions'
paws drumming the sand,
wood-scraped hands.
Trembling tendons

stretched taut like a book
snapped shut. The earth
absorbed her dearth
of emotion. He looked

like a dinner plate shattered
but shining, halo-shards
gleaming. Frankincense and myrrh
on her mind, a battered

future soothed with balm,
incense burning to calm.

Saint Mary Magdalen

In response to Saint Mary Magdalen surrounded by Angels, *a terracotta relief housed at Museum of Fine Arts, Boston.*

Strands of my hair and each band of my dress
are pressed into this baked clay with permanent
wave. Always they will sway as though
I stand in the wind. But I sag like melted wax.
My nose has fallen from my face. My hands
are snapped at the wrist. I am the woman
pinned to the street by an in-law
while her husband slices her ears from her head.
I wear a halo. The angel on whose forehead
my foot rests has wide eyes
snared in death.

Place du Vieux-Marché

In response to Jules Eugène Lenepveu's Joan of Arc at the Stake
in Rouen.

As a bird shines, comes
shooting from the clouds,
the executioner reaches his hand
to the ground searching for
the torch, burning now—
a log in camp when
she commanded the men.

See another man hoist
branches over his head,
kindling for the fire,
a cross on his chest,
and the priest kneeling—
he chants prayers.

A child asks, *What now?*
when the murder is over
and ashes are gathered.
What now? A small hand
pulling at the brown sleeve
of a threadbare dress.
Chores and dinner.

Life still happens after
the fire or gunshot.
Butter snaps in the pan.
Pots simmer with rice.
The dauphin holds his ring
under the light, smiles.

Elegy in Yellow

Boston Marathon Bombings

Three yellow balloons loosened from a hand,
a child in the crowd caught in the gasp
      of smoke and nails, shrapnel,
biting impalements—a punctured shin,
a sliced toe, and the sandal left shredded,
discarded like a bread crust on the table.
      Terror! Terror! Terror!
Each balloon is an alarming mouth
and this is the entrance to some sort of hell.
And this is the management of heaven:
running toward hell to tourniquet a knee.

Poem for My Young Cousins

The world will not mold
itself to fit your beliefs.
Learn early how to disagree
and harbor your own thoughts—
able boats roped to a steady dock.
Learn also how to board one
of these sloops and sail out,
how to hoist a salted canvas
in the wind and determine
your direction. Learn distance.
At night the sky is a sliced
wine bottle opened on a hinge.
Stars seem as close as an outstretched
thumb. Learn how to draw your arm
back to your chest and still feel
that shining presence.

The Wanting

It is not that I am tired.
It is that the pine trees lie to me
in eight tongues. With each scrape of branch
against needle, cells die in the roots.
I can cite nothing to prove this.
It is that the drunk last night
at the game spilled three-quarters of a cup
on my coat and shouted, *Skate!*,
showed the ring in his tongue when
he shouted, *Skate! Skate hard!*
The floor vibrated with his call.
It is that each retired number
hung from the rafters like a marked moon,
a printed thumb. One of the forwards
tilted his head when he shot the puck
and I thought about us. It is that
you could translate each fib and set down
the truth on white sheets of paper.
It is that your clean tongue has swiped
my mouth and has marked me, too.

Answers

Why do I hate cities
smelling of women and urine?

Is there anything in the world sadder
than a train standing in the rain?
—Pablo Neruda

The filth of the city
smelling of urine and men,
businessmen dressed in suits and shoes
they have shined on side streets,

the box and brush left behind
when the shoeshiners go home
to small houses built close
to old railroads, and no, Neruda,

nothing much is sadder
than trains standing in the rain
seen from ripped screens
behind stained windows

while the business meeting
in the historic restaurant
is going well, very well,
another batch of crisp cash

guaranteed in by the time
the shined shoes reach home
on the shelf beside the door,
then the man trips upstairs

unknotting his tie, his wife
rolls over and sighs,
I drank so much wine,
darling, waiting for you.

Leopard Tattoo

Nana's brother returned from WWII
with it inked on his arm, stretched
from shoulder blade to elbow—*a horrible
thing, its tongue sticking out.* He later
hid it under long-sleeve shirts.

He brought his niece with him
to the bar and bought her endless sodas
while he did shots, held cold beers
in his damp palms. The bar clock

ticked gunshots. He sang in the street
one night going home, slurred and loud,
so all would know—*Someone
died although he seems alive.*

Kissing the War Goodbye

In response to Alfred Eisenstaedt's V-J Day in Times Square. Kissing the War Goodbye *is the title of Victor Jorgensen's photograph of the same scene.*

Her hand is not wrapped around
his neck. It pushes against his chest.
Her chin, as he pulls her toward him,
pulls away. She guessed where he
had been. The Battle of Midway, maybe.
She tasted beer on his tongue and the kiss
lasted too long, should not have happened,
anyway. Another soldier smiled
and laughed walking past.
It was like kissing the war.
When she squirmed from his grasp,
she knew she had kissed a mouth
that knew violence, knew how to take.

The Red Vineyard

In response to Vincent van Gogh's The Red Vineyards Near Arles.

From the ground of blue
sounds, vines rise.
A horse harnessed to plow
waits for the man, seated,
slouched, to resume.

Women work in long dresses.
Heat gleams sweat on their faces.
In the farmhouse under the sun,
beside a tree almost green,
the daughter sleeps,

dreams of a bird wing and pancakes
in a basket. Shouts and songs ring
from the women outside.
Shadows spider the wall
when she wakes.

The Order

All in a row, ecclesiastical—
the nuns are veiled maids. Weather
and age wipe the *pretty* away

from this wall of headstones
no higher than the shin—
sun-bleached, whitewashed, thin.

The summer afternoon is a shroud.
Wind whistles over round stones,
lifts a sleeve from the arm.

The priest is a *prima donna,*
ten-foot-tall Latin cross polished
and shining like a gold dollar.

Shadowed on the stones
are the little maids who bend
and nod—*He leads the way.*

Girl Reading a Letter

In response to Johannes Vermeer's Girl Reading a Letter at an
Open Window.

To offer praise, not complain
that her life will be too soon

consumed with children and dishes,
soap bubbles that rise against a slate sky

and pop, saucers stained red with jam,
stale crumbs from the bread she bought.

To praise the upturned hat of fruit
spilling onto her bed, each apple

holding the shine or shadow of wind.
She has been in the orchard with her friend.

Praise that her hands hold the letter,
that the window is open, and sun comes in.

ENDNOTES

Discovering: *Dreams* is a painting by Sir Frederic William Burton.

Inside a Waterborne Canoe: The italicized line is from Anne Sexton's "The Starry Night."

Noon: After Jane Hirshfield's "The Heat of Autumn."

Metaphors: "Red of desire, red of hurt" is adapted from "White of forgetfulness, / of desecration" and "White of forgetfulness, / white of safety" (Louise Glück, "Persephone the Wanderer").

Blue Thread: The italicized line is from Yusef Komunyakaa's "Report from the Skull's Diorama."

Elizabeth: The following lines are from Anne Sexton's work. From "Lullaby," "My sleeping pill is white. / It is a splendid pearl." From "For the Year of the Insane," "although I am ugly, / submerged in my own past / and my own madness." From "Cripples and Other Stories," "I see dead rats in the toilet. / I'm one of the lunatics."

Place du Vieux-Marché: After Czeslaw Milosz's "Campo dei Fiori."

Answers: The epigraphs are from Pablo Neruda's *The Book of Questions*, translated by William O'Daly.

Jennifer LeBlanc earned an MFA in Creative Writing from Lesley University where she focused on feminist and ekphrastic poetry as well as traditional poetic forms and dramatic monologues. She also received a BA in English from Regis College in Weston, Massachusetts. *Descent* is her first full-length book, and individual poems have been published in journals such as *The Adirondack Review, CAIRN, The Main Street Rag,* and *Melusine.* Jennifer was nominated for a 2013 Pushcart Prize and works in the English Department at Tufts University.